IMAGES
of America

VACAVILLE

IMAGES
of America

VACAVILLE

Jerry Bowen

ARCADIA
PUBLISHING

Published by Arcadia Publishing
Charleston, South Carolina

Library of Congress Catalog Card Number: 2004104610

For all general information contact Arcadia Publishing at:
Telephone 843-853-2070
Fax 843-853-0044
E-mail sales@arcadiapublishing.com
For customer service and orders:
Toll-Free 1-888-313-2665

Visit us on the Internet at www.arcadiapublishing.com

An Apache Indian, Lorenzo Trujillo, was hired to guide the wagon train carrying the Vacas and Penas from New Mexico to Los Angeles.

CONTENTS

ACKNOWLEDGMENTS

One of the nice things about Vacaville is that so many organizations cooperate closely with each other when it comes to historical information. Even though most of the photographs used in this book came from the Vacaville Heritage Council and its contributing members Robert Allen and Ruth Holtz, a majority of the same photo collections are also available at the Vacaville Museum, a center for Solano County history located on historic Buck Avenue.

Often one organization will have a better negative or original photo than the other and is always willing to supply the best product for a project. Knowledge of the history of Solano County is obviously a winner because of such cooperation. This book was no different and I would like to thank museum director Shawn Lum for the ready access to the museum's files, and staff members Annie Farley and Heidi Casebolt who processed all requests.

The Vacaville Reporter newspaper, owned for many decades and only recently sold by the Rico family, has also been a keeper of local lore by means of regularly published history articles and special editions. In addition, the family has contributed thousands of negatives and photographs to the museum and the Vacaville Heritage Council. These have been invaluable in archiving the past. Old timers frequently drop by to identify the people and history behind the photographs, further contributing to the local knowledge base. Another helpful resource is the Solano County Genealogy Society, whose extensive files and records are always a valuable asset when researching local and family history. I would also like to thank DCS photography for advancing a copy of the official photograph of the current Vacaville City Council. In addition, I must acknowledge Carol Noske's in-depth and indispensible research on the history of Vacaville churches.

When it comes to longtime residents, the many old family albums, interviews, and stories contributed by them have been a continuing source of local histories. It's easy to understand why I consider Vacaville one of the more important sources of history of Solano County.

INTRODUCTION

In 1842 Manuel Vaca and Juan Felipe Pena came from New Mexico to California and settled near Putah Creek, then called the Lihuaytos River or Lihuaytos Creek. They applied jointly for and were granted a ten-league (one league equals about 4,500 acres) Mexican land grant called Lihuaytos. In actuality, due to the vague description of the boundaries, it actually covered in excess of 20 leagues overlapping the Rio de los Putos grant belonging to William Wolfskill.

On August 21, 1850, Juan Manuel Vaca sold a square English league of land, which is actually nine square miles, for $3,000 to William McDaniel with the provision that one square mile be designated as a new town of Vacaville. In addition, McDaniel was to deed back to Vaca 1,055 lots in the new town. Vaca, who spoke no English, thought he was only selling one square mile of land.

McDaniel had made an arrangement with lawyer Lansing B. Mizner that he would deed over half of the land in the deal with Vaca to Mizner in exchange for laying out the city and tending to the legal paper work. Mizner was fluent in both Spanish and English and acted as interpreter for the transaction with Vaca.

Juan Manuel Vaca, pictured at left, came from New Mexico to California in 1842. Juan Felipe Pena, at right, and Juan Manuel Vaca were jointly given a ten-league Mexican land grant called Lihuaytos.

While translating, it isn't clear if Mizner made it understandable to Vaca how much actual property was involved. The deed was written only in English instead of both languages. During translation, it isn't known if the term "one English league" (about nine square miles) was used or if the actual boundaries laid out in the deed were made clear. At any rate, the deal was made and Vaca placed his "X" on it. In 1851 Mizner laid out the new town of Vacaville, and McDaniel deeded the required lots to Vaca.

When Vaca discovered McDaniel was preparing to sell large portions of the other eight square miles at a tidy profit he informed McDaniel that the way he had understood the deal was that he had only sold one square mile, which was to become the town of Vacaville.

Vaca placed an ad in the *California Gazette* in May 1851 stating, "Caution. I hereby notify all persons not to purchase any lands from William McDaniel, which he claims to have purchased from me under title that he obtained under false pretenses and I shall institute suit against him to annul the title so fraudulently obtained by him. [Signed] Manual Baca [Vaca]."

McDaniel had been in negotiation with a couple of buyers with cash in hand. After reading Vaca's notice in the newspaper, the buyers informed McDaniel that they did not want to buy a lawsuit along with the land and backed out of the deal. McDaniel filed a libel lawsuit against Vaca and the case went to trial on October 30, 1851, before Judge Robert Hopkins.

Vaca hired the firm Jones, Tomkins & Stroube to represent him, the same firm that had bungled his land grant case before the land commission on his first application to ratify the grant according to the Treaty of Hidalgo provisions.

Vaca lost the case and the jury handed down a judgment on October 31, 1851, awarding McDaniel the sum of $16,750. Vaca filed an appeal to the state supreme court. After reviewing the evidence, the supreme court set aside the judgment against Vaca on February 5, 1852. In their opinion there was no malice in the notice. In addition, the lower court's proceedings were rife with sustained objections and overrulings that had no place in law, as well as other monumental mistakes in the proceedings. It is not certain if Vaca ever filed suit against McDaniel for the alleged fraudulent deal.

Vacaville was laid out and a map filed with the county on December 13, 1851. Vacaville started to grow as settlers began arriving. It is interesting to note that not even the original map was followed with its Spanish-named streets. The original trail into Vacaville had much to do with this as did the future property owners for whom the streets were eventually named.

By the 1960s, the Pena Adobe was in very bad condition when the Solano County Historical Society began restoration of the old structure.

One

VACAVILLE'S BEGINNING

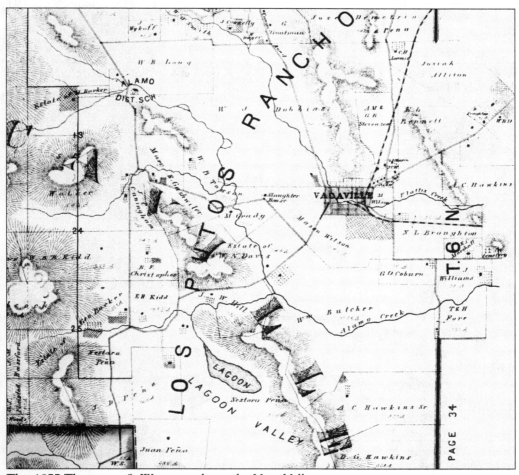

This 1877 Thompson & West map shows the Vaca Valley.

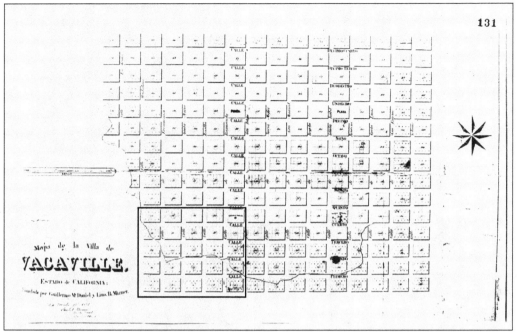

Lansing Mizner filed the Vacaville plat map in 1850. A total of 1,057 lots were deeded to Vaca; the streets all had Spanish names and the town sported two separate plazas.

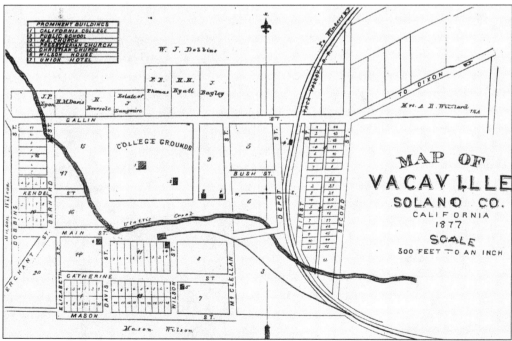

The 1877 Thompson & West map of Vacaville shows that the original plat map agreed upon by McDaniel and Vaca was never followed. The framed-in section of the top illustration corresponds to the lower illustration.

With the gold rush in full swing, many miners passed through the lush valleys surrounding Vacaville and many later returned to plant orchards and raise cattle. Large ranches were developed and Vacaville became a center of activity.

The Levi Korn Ranch was one of the many ranches in the area by the 1870s.

11

The two-story Luzena Wilson Hotel dominated the area. It was sold in 1874 to Col. E.S. "Ike" Davis, who added one of the first fire-sprinkler systems in the West. A water tank on the roof fed the fire suppression system. The building survived several major fires until it was destroyed during a blaze that wiped out the business district on the north side of Main Street, then crossed Main Street at the Ulatis Creek Bridge and burned the hotel. Colonel Davis died the day before the fire and it is believed his body may have been inside the hotel when it destroyed the structure. Today the Walker Opera House that was built in 1898 still occupies the site while

Davis Street lies between the hotel and the building to the left. The fence line and dirt road at the bottom of the photo is the approximate location of today's Monte Vista Avenue. The wide road with the small wooden bridge later became Bernard Street and the road to the right—later realigned parallel with Bernard—is today's Dobbins Street. The fence line above the wide road in the center of the photo is today's Elizabeth Street. The second building to the right of the fence line is the Gillespie Store, Wells Fargo Station, and Pony Express stop. It later served as a warehouse before it was finally torn down. Today the Heritage Café occupies the site.

13

One of the first merchandise stores to open in Vacaville was the E.F. Gillespie Store in 1854. In 1857 Wells Fargo opened an express and post-office agency in the same building, with E.F. Gillespie as the agent. In addition, it served as a Pony Express stop in 1865.

After being used as a warehouse for several years, Gillespie's store fell into disrepair and was gone before 1897, possibly destroyed by one of the many major fires in Vacaville before the turn of the century.

One of the two locomotives owned by the Vaca Valley & Clear Lake Railroad is shown here leaving its barn in 1869. The railroad was an important link to Vacaville's growth.

E.S. Davis, owner of the Davis Hotel (formerly the Luzena Wilson Hotel) poses proudly in front of his hotel about 1883. The Davis Hotel boasted a total of 27 rooms upstairs, a beautiful two-acre park, and was fitted with a commodious bathroom where dusty travelers were sure to appreciate the opportunity to actually bathe. Young men stand perilously on top of the Good Templars Hall across the street. All the buildings on both sides of the street were destroyed by fire in November 1888. Davis had died the day before and was lying in state in the hotel. It is not certain if his body was still in the hotel when it was destroyed.

No one could have known that disaster awaited when this ad for the former Luzena Wilson Hotel, then known as the Davis Hotel, touted its facilities in an 1888 issue of *California Illustrated*.

Bob Cernon (left) and Constable Joe Stadfelt pose on Main Street near the corner of Davis Street on the remains of a wagon disabled by the mud created by rains shortly after water mains were installed in 1885.

Only wooden walks kept the occasional visitor at the Vaca Valley Hotel from getting stuck in the mud created by rainy weather shortly after the new water mains were installed on Main Street in 1885. The Vaca Valley Hotel was renamed the Raleigh Hotel after Raleigh Barcar bought it.

During the early growing season, the Vacaville Train Depot was a busy place with the loading of fruit, as shown in this 1887 image.

Refrigerated train cars were an innovation of the growers in Solano County and contributed to the widespread shipping of the area's products.

Stately homes were built on the ranches as a result of the excellent profits earned from fruit orchards. The Rogers home on Buck Avenue was built in 1892. The Vacaville Museum occupies this site today.

Many wagon makers opened for business in Vacaville during its early days as a result of the bustling fruit industry. J.A. Collier was located near Depot Street, one of the busiest areas of town from the 1880s to the turn of the century.

Main Street wasn't exactly the busiest place in the world when this photograph was taken in 1888. A team and wagon are parked in front of the Crystal Building, now occupied by Amphlett's Interiors, Main St. Salon, and Tux-n-Tailor Bridal. This building is one of the oldest brick structures in Vacaville.

The W.B. Parker Ranch was located south of today's Merchant Street. Parker planted his orchard in 1878 and it came into bearing in 1885. The ranch became one of Vacaville's earliest developments and today Elm School is located on the site.

This 1888 view of the Vacaville Train Depot was taken from a cornfield to the east. A wood-burning stove heated the depot. In the background are the Cash Store and Mrs. Miller's Hotel.

George Akerly bought the bankrupt Chittenden business shortly after graduating from high school and opened a store at this location on the corner of Davis and Main Streets in 1888. Akerly's slogan was "If you can't find it at Akerly's, there's no use looking further." The Masonic Lodge occupied the upper floor. After selling this building to A.A. Collier, Akerly moved his business to a larger location on the corner of Main and Dobbins Streets. This photo was taken around 1905.

Both Reid's Drug Store and Trent Hewitt's Jewelry were located in the same room. R.L Reid is shown on the left and J.K. Buck or Ike Blum is standing in center. Trent Hewitt Sr. is leaning on the counter to the right and Trent Hewitt Jr., the storeowner, is behind the counter.

In this 1892 image, looking west across Depot Street, California College and the belfry of the grammar school are visible in the background. The college operated from 1865 to 1895 in two different locations; the grammar school operated from 1885 to 1908.

Eastern newspaper editors visit Vacaville on May 21, 1892. Because of Vacaville's early growing season the region became nationally known for its great bounty of fruit. People would consequently come to Vacaville from all over the country, especially from the East, to tour the area.

Dr. and Mrs. Dobbins enjoy a buggy ride near their home on Dobbins Street near the intersection of today's Dobbins and Monte Vista Streets.

Even though the earthquake of 1892 shook down the front sections of all the brick buildings along Main Street, the structures were in good enough condition to be saved. The facades were rebuilt and still exist today as part of Vacaville's historic downtown. Earthquake damage to the two-story Odd Fellows building and the other businesses along the south side of Main Street was limited mainly to the front of the structures.

Akerly's store is shown here after the earthquake in 1892. The structure eventually became a warehouse for Basic Foods and was finally torn down. The KUIC Radio Plaza building occupies the site today.

Vacaville's oldest structure on Main Street, the Crystal Building on the corner of Main and Dobbins, sustained major damage during the earthquake in 1892. It was repaired and housed many businesses right up to and including today.

The rear of the Crystal Building, which housed the public library and post office, was severely damaged in the 1892 earthquake.

Early Solano County pioneers gathered on April 29, 1894 to celebrate J.M. Pleasants's 85th birthday. Shown in this rare photograph of many of the earliest Vacaville pioneers are, from left to right, (front row) John Reid Wolfskill, M.R. Miller, James Madison Pleasants, W.R. Gibbs, Jim Collins, and G.W. Thissel; (back row) William James Pleasants, E.R. Thurber, Richard Long, and E. Rust.

By 1894 the Pena Adobe had become the residence of Jesus Tapia Rivera. The original adobe structure had been covered over with a wooden shell and additional living space had been created. Shown, from left to right, are Jesus Tapia Rivera, Grace Diaz (who later married Phillip Pena), and Rivera's wife, Nestora (Pena).

26

The Chinese section of Vacaville on Dobbins and Kendal Streets suffered many fires over the years. Each time the residents rebuilt with closely spaced wooden buildings that made the area a prime candidate for more destruction. This view of the Chinese section after 1900 shows that the condition continued into the 20th century.

The Vacaville Land Agency offered 200 acres of choice fruit-producing land near Vacaville at eight percent interest.

THE CHANCE OF A LIFE-TIME!

Special Long Credit Sale of Fine Fruit and Vine Land

IN PEACEFUL GLEN VALLEY, SOLANO COUNTY,

Three Miles from the Flourishing Town of Vacaville

By G. N. PLATT & SONS,

OF THE

VACAVILLE LAND AGENCY—The Leading Real Estate Firm in Solano County.

We are now prepared to offer in addition to a large line of choice Suburban and Village Property,

---200 Acres of Choice Land Situated in Peaceful Glen Valley---

(Immediately Adjoining the well-known Ranch of the late Jesse McGowan.)

This property will be sold in Sub-Divisions to suit, on the most Liberal Terms, Long Credit and Law Rate of Interest. On all lots sold before August 1, 1888, we shall require 6 months' interest at 8 per cent. per annum. paid in advance, which will be the only payment required up to Feb. 1, 1889. Payments thereafter will consist of interest paid semi-annually, in advance, until EIGHT SUCH PAYMENTS HAVE BEEN MADE. At the time of the payment of the 9th semi-annual interest, one-fourth of the purchase price of the land will be required in addition to the interest, and the balance due shall be paid in 3 EQUAL ANNUAL PAYMENTS, with interest payable annually. On lots purchased after Aug. 1, 1888, the first payment shall consist of interest from date of Purchase up to Feb. 1st, 1889, and 6 months' interest in addition thereto. All interest must be paid Aug. 1st and Feb. 1st of each year. A liberal discount will be allowed to persons who wish to pay the principal sooner than above designated.

IN ADDITION TO THE ABOVE, WE WILL ALSO OFFER

100 Acres of Improved Land, Partly set to Trees and Vines

also on the Tract a good nearly new modern house; good barn and outbuildings; good wells of water; fine location.

On this Improved Land one-Fourth of purchase price must be paid down, and the balance in three equal annual payments, with interest at 8 per cent.

This property is situated within three miles of Vacaville and within one mile of the Railroad Station, on the Hartley Tract. There is a good school within one-fourth mile of the property, and persons buying here will find a good neighborhood of kind and enterprising people. To persons seeking a profitable investment or desirous of purchasing a small home in the country with charming scenery, good soil, delightful climate, and an UNUSUALLY EASY TERMS, this is the most favorable opportunity ever offered in the State. Communication with San Francisco and Sacramento by rail twice each day.

No safer investment can be made than to secure property so favorably located in this delightful section of the country.

Persons can satisfy themselves that this land will produce good trees and vines by examining those already on the improved portions of the property, or on ranches adjacent.

G. N. Platt & Sons will be pleased to furnish any further information desired in regard to this property, and will show the land to intending purchasers free of charge.

27

New businesses entered the scene toward the end of the 19th century, including Frank C. Chapman's Harness Shop on Main Street, which sported a unique sign when it was built. A devastating fire that started in the harness shop in November 1888 destroyed most of the buildings on the north side of Main Street to the Ulatis Bridge. Kappel & Kappel Realty occupies this site today on the northwest corner of Main and Dobbins Streets.

Vacaville's newspaper started up in 1883 and by 1898 occupied its own building, which was named after owner Raleigh Barcar, who bought the paper in 1892.

Jim Miller's drug store was located on Merchant and Main Streets in the Triangle Building. The son of M.R. Miller, Jim Miller began business in 1877. In 1884 he strung Vacaville's first telephone line from his store to Elmira. The boy behind the counter is Fred Deacon, and Jim Miller is shown in front.

New telephone wire was in the process of being strung on Main Street in 1900 as Vacaville entered the 20th century. By 1901 Vacaville had a grand total of 110 telephones.

By the turn of the century, Main Street bore little evidence of the 1892 earthquake's destruction, and most of the buildings appeared much as they do today. Walker Opera House on the corner of Davis and Main Streets was built in 1897 on the empty lot that had been vacant since the Davis Hotel burned down, and across the street Akerly's store had been repaired. Somehow the rickety old wooden bridge across Ulatis Creek managed to survive the earthquake, but wagons crossing it were required to do no more than three miles per hour because of the possibility of collapse. The bridge was finally replaced in 1912 with a concrete structure still in use today.

Two

THE FRUITFUL YEARS

Peaches are dipped and peeled at the H.A. Bassford Ranch.

From the comfort of a shade tree in the late 1880s, Mrs. Elise P. Buckingham views her Lagoon Valley Ranch from the hills west of the valley.

Fresh from college, Mrs. Buckingham's son Thomas Hugh Buckingham efficiently managed his mother's Lagoon Valley Ranch and turned it into a very profitable business.

Mrs. Elise P. Buckingham is shown in her living room around 1885. The home was built by the Pena family and paid for with cattle hides and tallow. It was constructed from lumber cut in Maine, individually numbered, and shipped around the Horn. The house remained standing for over 100 years but was eventually torn down for scrap.

The Buckingham Fruit Label became well known on the East Coast because it identified boxes of fruit known for freshness and delicious taste.

Vacaville was one of the first areas to ship fruit in refrigerated railroad cars. Shown here is the Earl Fruit Company shipping shed on Main Street with a nearby refrigerated railroad car.

Another shipping shed on East Main Street was the Pinkham/McKevitt operation. Shown on the loading platform, from left to right, are Marion Brazelton, Elmer Waggoner, Schmicky, Lee Hardesty, Burt Wykoff, and Henry Simpers. Frank B. McKevitt Jr. is making boxes.

It was always a busy time when loading fruit for the Eastern market. This photo was taken from the top of the Vacaville Train Depot at the north end of Depot Street in 1895.

On May 21, 1892, Vacaville residents and ranchers provided transportation to show off the great fruit orchards of Vaca Valley to newspaper editors visiting from the East.

Entertainment was provided when relatives of F.N. Wertner from New Bedford, Massachusetts, visited his ranch in 1888.

Workers at the Chubb Ranch, once located on Vaca Valley Road, were busy dipping prunes and grading them before placing them on trays for drying when this photo was taken in 1905.

Elegant homes were built as a result of productive fruit orchards, evidenced by this 1886 photograph of the W.W. Smith residence on the Ulatis Ranch north of Vaca Valley Road.

Elegant homes weren't the only result of Vaca Valley's productive fruit orchards. Pictured here is the W.W. Smith barn.

One of the most successful fruit producers of the area was Frank. H. Buck. His facilities included this apricot drying yard in what was known as "Bucktown" north of Vaca Valley Road and along Pleasants Valley Road.

Frank H. Buck employed many workers on his ranch on Bucktown Road. Many of them are shown in this photo at a Bucktown packing shed preparing to load boxes of fruit for shipment. The packing shed was destroyed by fire in 1931.

Helen Davis earned celebrity status as a winning harness racer. Her horses also served double duty, delivering dried fruit for the Buck Company. Shown here is a pair of her racehorses, Sire and Dam, around 1933. In the wagon is Helen Davis, who dressed in men's clothing for the arduous work.

Frank H. Buck's enterprises afforded him the luxury of having many employees at his mansion on Buck Avenue in Vacaville. Shown here are his Chinese houseboys in native costume.

These homes on Buck Avenue reflected the good years of fruit production in the Vacaville area.

UPPER LEFT: the W.W. Smith house was originally built in 1893 for the Pinkhoms. Smith bought it in 1913 and fire destroyed it in 1979.

UPPER CENTER: The Frank H. Buck home was built by George Sharpe in 1890. A brick veneer was added in 1930. Frank H. Buck Sr. died in 1916 and his son Frank H. Buck Jr. took over the family business.

UPPER RIGHT: George Sharpe built the J.H. Rogers house in 1892 for $5,000. The house was demolished in 1963 and the Vacaville Museum stands on the site today.

LEFT CENTER: This home was built for saloonkeeper Mr. Ray Bennett. It was destroyed by fire in the 1940s and a new home was constructed by William Cole, a local manager for the Southern Pacific Railroad.

RIGHT CENTER: The George W. Crystal home was built in 1893 by George Sharpe.

LOWER LEFT: William Henry Buck, a first cousin of Frank H. Buck, built this home in 1892 for $5,000. The house was completely renovated in 2003.

LOWER CENTER: Shown here is the C.N. Hartley home.

LOWER RIGHT: This home was built in 1892 for prominent rancher and businessman H.D. Chandler.

Three

BOOM AND BUST YEARS

Shortly after the turn of the century, wagons, stagecoaches, and newfangled automobiles shared the streets of Vacaville.

In 1907 Ulatis Stables occupied the corner of Bernard and Main Streets. G.A. Powers Blacksmith Shop is to the right, across the street.

According to the clock in this photo, it was 8:20 when this view of Main Street, looking east, was taken in 1908. In the buildings to the right are a millinery shop, the *Vacaville Reporter* office, J.M. Coffman's Ice Cream Parlor, and a candy store. The post office was located in the Triangle Building. The sign on the Triangle Building reads "Schaffer's Hats and Clothing."

This 1909 view of Main Street looking west shows the following businesses: Edstrom's, Arnold and Bisbee Hardware, and Laughlin Lumber on the near left; and Reid's Drug Store in the Triangle Building farther down the street. On the right, the large two-story building housed Akerly's store on the bottom floor at the northeast corner of Dobbins and Main Streets. The old plaza bandstand on the corner of Bernard and Main Streets is visible on the right.

This hotel was originally built in 1884 by E.P. Williams and named the Western Hotel. It was sold in 1888 and renamed the Brunswick Hotel, then passed through the hands of several more owners. At one time it was named the Vaca Valley Hotel, as seen here. In 1901 Raleigh Barcar bought the building and named it the Raleigh Hotel.

These three photos provide a panoramic view of Vacaville from the tower of the old high school in 1908 looking down Main Street. This view shows Main, Wilson, and Catherine Streets. The Catholic church is on the right and the Christian church is to the left on the corner of Wilson and Catherine Streets.

This view includes the town hall, Akerly's store, the opera house, Edstrom's, Arnold and Bisbee Hardware, Laughlin Lumber, Bennett's Saloon, the IOOF building, Triangle Building, and the old wooden bridge over Ulatis Creek.

This view of the west side of town includes the Triangle Building, the Crystal Building, the Masonic Building, the Raleigh Hotel, and the steeple of the Presbyterian church.

Vacaville's jail is visible in the foreground as the small building next to Ulatis Creek. A story is told of a pair of drunks who, while occupying the two flimsy cells, disassembled a portion of the jail and stacked the wood neatly before making their escape. Early one morning in 1906, the jail was found shoved into the creek. Vacaville citizens were glad to see it destroyed, and jokingly pointed fingers at the Lady's Town Improvement Society as the culprit. Vacaville Town Hall, one of the first reinforced concrete structures in the West, was constructed to take the jail's place, opening its doors in 1907. Today the Vacaville Heritage Council and Solano County Genealogy Society occupy the building.

Town Hall, Vacaville, Cal.

45

V.F.D.

S. W. Bentley.
Chief

J. C. Duncan. Foreman.
Bert Evans, 1st Asst Foreman.
R. Cannon. 2nd Asst Foreman.
J.W. Duncklon. Clerk.
C. R. Bugbee. Treasurer.
Stewards.
H. Baucom, M. Cline.

Fire Police.
C. E. Lawrence, Fred Ream.
G. A. Mauer, Jas. Sullivan.

Nozzlemen.
C. R. Bugbee, V. Radcliffe.
G. P. Akerly, C. O. Hawkins.

Hydrantmen.
R. H. Platt. Wm. Strong.

Hook & Ladder Men.
H. Baucom, S. W. Bentley.
M. T. Jewell. B. K. Gill.
E. Lawrence. C. A. Foutz.

Extra - Men.
E. Waggoner. Wm. De Haven.
C. Hyde. A. C. Beelard.

1909.

In the early days fires often devoured major sections of towns while town trustees too often ignored the genuine need for an efficient fire department with proper equipment, or the town coffers simply could not support the needs of firefighters. Vacaville was no different. This early roster of volunteer firemen shows that the interest in fire protection was at least present. By 1909, after conflagrations repeatedly destroyed fire-prone buildings, volunteers finally began to make some, although not fully adequate, progress. The items below are a small reminder of the equipment firefighters used, in addition to a hose cart and chemical fire extinguishers that were strategically placed around town in 1909.

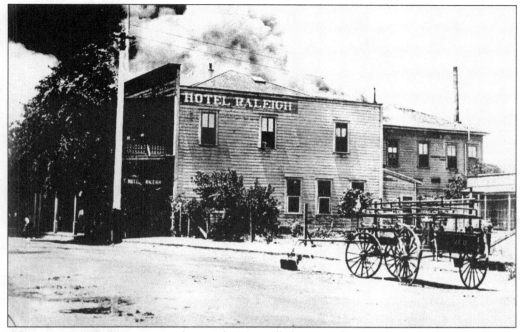

After surviving numerous major fires in the Vacaville business district, the Raleigh House finally succumbed to flames on July 11, 1909. The heat from the fire was so intense the Presbyterian church steeple across the street began burning. Note that the hose cart, Vacaville's only major firefighting equipment, was useless because no water was available. The first permanent Vacaville Post Office was built on the site in 1938.

An empty lot is all that remained of the Hotel Raleigh after it burned in 1909. In a spectacular show of courage, Guy Bassett, George Akerly, and C.E. Lawrence managed to save the Presbyterian church across the street by cutting the steeple loose and pulling it to the ground.

47

The first railroad built to Vacaville, the Vaca Valley & Clear Lake Railroad Company, was locally financed and connected to Elmira about five miles away in 1869. The depot was located near the middle of Depot Street opposite today's Kragen's Auto Store. Southern Pacific took over the railroad in later years. This photo was taken around the turn of the century.

A wood-burning stove heated the inside of the Southern Pacific Depot on Depot Street. William D. Cole stands in the corner and Lester Parker is next to stove in this 1912 photo.

A wagon crosses the newly constructed bridge over Ulatis Creek in 1912. Vacaville High School is in the background on the left and the grammar school is on the right. Town engineer Frank Steiger, who also designed the old town hall, designed the Ulatis Bridge; both are still in use today. The Ulatis Bridge created an important link between the central commercial district and the outlying ranches and orchards around Vacaville. Originally the bridge was constructed of wood to accommodate horse-drawn wagons and foot traffic. Years later it became necessary to walk wagons across the rickety bridge.

Until 1915, Vacaville had to rely on temporary locations for a library. Finally, after several years of dedicated effort, the Vacaville Saturday Club received a grant for a permanent Carnegie Library. Many of the local citizens attended the grand opening ceremonies on July 17, 1915.

The Triangle Building was constructed in 1898 but not occupied until 1903 due to litigation. The triangle shape was used to take the best advantage of the land and the intersections of Merchant, Dobbins, and Main Streets. Many important businesses occupied the building in the early days, including Schaffer's Clothing, Dr. Leroy Towson's dental office, Dr. Palmer's medical practice, the L.M. Miller Drug store, the First National Bank, the U.S. Post Office, and the early telephone exchange.

George Akerly's new store and the telephone company were located in the bottom floor of the Masonic Building, constructed around the turn of the century on the northwest corner of Dobbins and Main Streets. The Masonic Temple, Dr. W.C. Jenny, and Cecelia Clark's Hair Dresser Shop occupied the upper floor. The building burned down in a spectacular fire in 1939.

50

In 1891, Vacaville had very little in the way of firefighting equipment due to a lack of action by the town trustees despite at least five major fires. Even with persistent efforts to establish a volunteer department, fund-raising efforts by the men, and fiery editorials describing the need in the *Vacaville Reporter*, very little in the way of efficient equipment for the times was obtained. With 10 percent of the county's population in Vacaville, the town's fire equipment consisted of a volunteer hose company, a hose cart, fire bombs (chemical-filled glass containers), water buckets strategically placed around downtown, and 13 fire hydrants with an unreliable water supply. On July 25, 1895, City Ordinance 41 was approved, establishing an official city fire department. The chief was to receive $50 a year and members of the fire department would be paid 25¢ per drill or meeting and 50¢ an hour while fighting fires. On September 8, 1895, another major fire struck downtown Vacaville that destroyed Main Street's north side buildings, including 12 businesses, Bowles Opera House, and 50 Chinese homes, barns, and outhouses. As a result, the trustees finally began paying a little more attention to the needs of the fire department. Improvement continued to be made until finally, with the new age of automobiles, Vacaville purchased a fire engine, which included 500 feet of fire hose and an electric siren, on January 14, 1917, from the Seagrave Company for $6,000. On the new fire engine, from left to right, are Russell Chandler, Frank Eversole, Joe Libonati, Ben Newell, and Earl Brazelton.

World War I interrupted the daily routine in Vacaville. Patriotic displays replaced celebrations. Here Helen Davis leads Red Cross volunteers during a parade in 1917 across Ulatis Bridge at the end of Main Street.

During a World War I bond rally in 1918, Red Cross volunteers, from left to right, posed for this photo: (front row) Uriel Rutherford, Agnes Johnson, Dulcie Hargis, and Pearl Evins; (back row) Lorena Evans, Cecelia Clark, Sadie Cowan, and Grace Cowan. The rally raised $7,772.50.

Many methods were used to raise money to support the war. A Liberty Bond train traveling across the nation made a stop at the loading sheds on East Main Street in early 1918.

Excited crowds began to gather around the Liberty Bond train while one of the new tanks being used in the war effort was unloaded. Vacaville constable Joseph Stadfeldt stands next to the man with the gun.

Vacaville citizens gathered around the displays on the Liberty Bond train to view the exhibits and buy war bonds.

Sons of the early pioneer Dobbins family, S.P. Dobbins Jr. and W.U. Stanley Dobbins, were among the many residents of Vacaville who enlisted in the U.S. Army during World War I.

In 1914, the Vacaville Post Office was located in the northwest corner of the Triangle Building. A bicycle shop occupies the space today.

In 1918, the telephone company was housed in the Masonic Building, as it was known, on the northeast corner of Main and Dobbins Streets.

Today it is a private home, but it was once known as the Elizabeth Street Hospital, serving Vacaville residents for many years before a regular hospital was built. A plaque in front of the building marks its historic significance.

The Japanese business section flourished from the 1920s to the late 1930s on the west side of Dobbins Street between Kendall and Monte Vista Streets, but it went into decline in the early 1940s. Shown here, from the left, are the following businesses: Kimoto-ya boarding house, Mishi's Beauty Salon, Nakamura's Store, Ichimoto's Confectionery, a pool hall, a barber shop, Oni-san's (Okabata) Tavern, and the Makino family's ABC Company market. This section was torn down in 1944 and replaced by part of a federal housing project.

The Fourth of July was always a good reason to put on a parade. This 1920 photograph was taken on Main Street looking west, with the Crystal Building and Triangle Building on the right.

When the Lincoln Highway passed through Vacaville, travelers had to cross over the notable Vaca Valley Bridge. Then it was still a few minutes down the road on what is today's Merchant Street to get to Vacaville proper. The bridge was located on today's Butcher Road over Alamo Creek near the I-80 Alamo Street exit.

By 1920 automobiles and dealerships were overtaking the old horse-and-buggy days as this photograph, looking west down Main Street, attests.

When the Raleigh Hotel burned down in 1909, Vacaville was without public lodging until the two-story, 34-room Vacaville Hotel on the corner of Merchant and Parker Streets opened for business in 1920. As luck would have it, that hotel would only last 16 years before it too was destroyed by fire in 1936.

In 1931, the labor movement gave rise to many heated demonstrations. Agitation from some elements, such as the Communist Party, often resulted in riots around the United States. This April 1, 1931 *Reporter* cartoon urged those elements to be expelled from the country.

Send Them Back, Uncle Sam! — By Albert T. Raid

Increased competition from the Central Valley and new government regulations spelled the decline of profits and the beginning of the end for the local fruit industry. Lower wages created more problems until striking fruit laborers took to the streets on December 9, 1932, to vent their frustration. Fueled by communist agitation and labor unions, about 300 protesters gathered in front of the Vacaville Carnegie Library on Main Street for speeches followed by a march down Main Street.

From the turn of the century to 1934, Vacaville's Main Street changed little other than the businesses that occupied the buildings.

After years of operating out of various temporary quarters, Vacaville finally built its first permanent U.S. Post Office on March 12, 1938. In the past, fires and earthquakes had destroyed some of the post offices. Opening day ceremonies were attended by many Vacaville citizens.

In 1939, a disastrous fire destroyed the Masonic Building on the northeast corner of Main and Dobbins Streets, claiming Akerly's General Store, the Masonic Temple, the Pacific Telephone and Telegraph office, Dr. Jenny's office, and Cecelia Clark's beauty shop. Damage totaled $150,000.

Akerly's locally famous motto, "If you can't find it at Akerly's, there's no use looking further," would never grace the streets of Vacaville again.

The great fruit business era gradually came to an end as remnants of the early days began to disappear. The fruit sheds and railroad tracks along East Main Street were dismantled as the 1940s approached. The icehouse that once stood at the end of these sheds is forever gone.

The Northern Electric V&N station near the intersection of Davis and Catherine Streets was shut down as the 1940s approached. Eventually all traces of the station and railroad tracks were removed. The railroad right-of-way survives today as a bicycle/walking trail through Vacaville on the south side of I-80.

Frank H. Buck was 16 when he arrived in California with his father, Leonard W. Buck. Over the years, he and his father built a respectable fruit business on about 700 acres of land in Vacaville. Later he expanded into other businesses around the state, including oil and land enterprises. He was one of the richest men in the area when he died in San Francisco in 1916.

COMPLIMENTS OF

FRANK H. BUCK

CONGRESSMAN

THIRD CONGRESSIONAL DISTRICT

Frank H. Buck Jr. was born and raised in Vacaville and entered into politics in 1932 as a Democrat, defeating Forrest Curry by a 20,000-vote margin. He was subsequently returned to Congress until 1942 when he once again ran for office, although at the time it appeared he might not win. His death forever decided the issue in October 1942, but he left behind a legacy of community service that still has an effect on Vacaville today.

The Nut Tree was almost completely hidden under the branches of the old black oak tree for which it was named in 1921.

By 1940 the Nut Tree fruit stand along Highway 40 had expanded considerably and become a Vacaville landmark. Members of the Power family were experts at marketing their delicacies to the traveler, running a business that was customer-oriented and could even be said to have strongly influenced the creation of California cuisine.

Four

THE EARLY SCHOOLS

Ulatis Academy, a private institution boasting separate boarding houses for boys and girls, opened in 1855 on a small rise on the south side of East Main Street between Wilson Avenue and McClellan Street. Inadequate funding caused the school to close in 1858. In 1861, the Methodist Episcopal Church South purchased the Ulatis Academy and opened it as Pacific Methodist College South, the first chartered college in the Sacramento Valley.

On October 13, 1865, the cornerstone was laid for the new Pacific Methodist College in today's Andrews Park. The college was relocated to Oakland on September 2, 1884, and the building was used as a private school. In 1892 an earthquake severely damaged the structure. Although it was declared unsafe the same year it was not dismantled until 1895. Most of the bricks were used to rebuild some of the buildings on North Main Street between Bernard Street and the Ulatis Creek Bridge after fire destroyed the original wooden structures on September 14, 1895. Some of these buildings are still in use today.

In 1885 the Normal and Scientific School (formerly the Baptist California College) shared "College Hill" with a new neighbor when Vacaville constructed its first urban grade school, Ulatis Grammar School, shown here on the right. The tower collapsed during the 1892 earthquake and was replaced with a shorter version.

The old Normal and Scientific School (formerly Baptist California College) was severely damaged in the 1892 earthquake. It was finally torn down in 1895 and replaced in 1898 by the new Vacaville High School, shown on the left, at a cost of about $10,000.

On July 4, 1898, Vacaville celebrated Independence Day with two parades on Main Street. The morning parade traveled east to west from Ulatis Creek with the theme "Remember the Maine." The noon parade was for kids only and celebrated the opening of the Vacaville High School that can be seen in the background.

This 1898 photograph shows the splendid Vacaville High School, designed by George Sharpe, shortly after its completion on College Hill, which is Andrews Park today. The school served Vacaville until July 30, 1954, when contractor Homer Arons of Sacramento demolished it.

Sports were always a high priority for Vacaville High School and the community. The 1901 football team members shown here are, from left to right, (front row) Steve Gambel, Lewis Marshall, Rolla Gray, and Elmer Graham; (middle row) Ed Bassford, James Hardie, Gabriel Higueira, and Wilford Robinson; (back row) Fred Coleman, Oscar Atkinson, Leroy Towson, and Alvin Weldon.

The 1905 Vacaville High School girls basketball team became the Northern California champions. It must have been tough playing in the area's heat in these uniforms. The members of the team, from left to right, are (front row) Laura Haggerty, Verna Dutton, and Ethel Parks; (back row) Barbara Reid, Iva Rogers, Willa Marshall, Fidelia Haggerty, Maude Sharpe, and Jane Burton.

Vacaville High School baseball team members in 1907 are, from left to right, (front row) Russell Chandler and Lawrence Killingsworth; (middle row) Sidney Hoyt, John Rugg, Harvey Syster, and Frank Jewett; (back row) Charles Rogers, Carl Hendricks, Mory Buck, and Wiley Killingsworth.

The 1909 Vacaville High School senior class included, from left to right, (top row) Belle Hagerty, Charles Rogers, and Erma Montgomery; (middle row) Esther Sharpe, Laurens Killingsworth, and Leonard W. Buck; (bottom row) Loraine Watson, Mae Farrell, and Roland E. Hartley Jr. When this class of only nine students graduated, Esther Sharpe wrote in the yearbook:

> *At last we are mighty Seniors, and although there are not many of our original class remaining, still we have tried to distinguish ourselves in different ways and a majority of us have prepared to enter the University.*
>
> *We now realize that we are about to begin a new and broader life, and although we look forward with eager anticipation to making a brilliant career for ourselves we can not but look back with regret upon the four happy years spent at V.H.S., to which we now say, Adios.*

In 1913 the entire student body of Vacaville High School was photographed on the school steps. The freshman class had 17 students, the sophomore class had 12, the junior class 4, and the senior class 13.

The Vacaville High School freshman class of 1941 saw many major changes as the clouds of World War II gathered. Many of the Japanese classmates were sent to internment camps and most did not return when the war ended.

In 1908 the first Ulatis Elementary School on College Hill had become too unstable because of damage caused by the 1892 earthquake. The school was torn down by original designer and builder George Sharpe, who then built this new Vacaville Grammar School on the same spot in the same year.

In 1909 seventh- and eighth-grade Ulatis Elementary School students gathered on the grass in front of the school for a group photograph.

The "Sunbonnet Babes" of Ulatis Elementary School posed for this photo in 1920. From left to right are (front row) Marion ?, Roberta Gates, Christine Peabody, Barbara Easton, Thelma McMillan, Benelle Rutherford, Dorothy Donald, and Norma Parks; (back row) Norma Peabody, Betty Little, Nola Cox, Eleth May, Anita Ream, and Wilma Johnson.

Consolidation of the school districts began in 1921. The district then bought an empty lot on the west side of Ulatis school and built the new 6-room, 400-seat auditorium Ulatis Elementary School on McClellan Street, dedicating it on July 28, 1923.

A new facility was constructed next to the old high school to accommodate the increasing number of students. This brick building containing five classrooms and a gym opened in 1930. It was destroyed in a devastating fire in August 1953.

In 1938 the Vaca Valley Drum and Bugle Corp posed for this picture in front of Vacaville High School. From left to right are (front row) Mike Ramos, John Campos, Lloyd Johnson, John Contreras, Meggi ?, Nelson Piper, Greta Neil, Jack Pritchett, Tom Williams, James Willson, Willie Estepa, Fred ?, John Ramos, Bert Shepard, Erna Tershuren, Fred ?, Mary Escano, Julian Codina (bass drum), Jacoba Lopez, Bob Damiano, Joe Lopez, Jack Hatanaka, Joe Moreno, Hall Clark, E.H. Padan, Hilten Reynolds, Collen Reynolds, and Patty Holmes; (back row) George Kirbyson, Charles Hoover, Martin Markowitz, Tony Pulido, Mary Hilden, Arther Leonard, Roland Eckert, Robert Young, Charles McCrory, Manuel Nofuentes, Brewster Chandler, David Mix, John Elasces, Kay Graft, Bud Bowles, Roy Puerta, Fred Bowles, John Pulido, Carmen ?, Bob Power, Jim Silva, Alice Nughi, Annie Grima, Mary Helen Power, and Carmen ?.

74

Knowledge of their culture was a high priority for the Japanese. This photograph, taken in 1938 in front of the Japanese school building located behind the Buddhist temple, includes the following: Kimiko Takao, Sumiko Yoshida, Susie Tsuda, Yoakemi Kimoto, Flora Togami, Hatsieyo Hatanaka, Sumiko Handa, Shigeka Nakamura, Fiemiko Wada, Emily Matsuo, Chiyuko Makino, Nancy Morishita, Keizo Kornura, Kazue Takao, Takashi Tsujita, Teruo Nakarnura, Minoru Sano, Shigeru Tsujita, Atao Mori, Fred Makino, Aiko Takimoto, Kiyomi Masuda, Kioko Teramaye, Misao Takimoto, Chizu Matsuura, Miyo Fujikawa, Mrs. Nukui, Clara Togami, Reverend Nukui, Sawaki Harada, M. Kawamoto, Masomi Tsujimoto, Mujoji Yamada, Minoru Sano, Hiroshi Takahashi, Hachiro Handa, Tomio Teraura, Yoshiko Fujikawa, Shizuy Takeda, Michiko Nishimoto, Babr Shimamoto, Emi Mori, Helen Kadowaki, Kaoru Matsuno, Umeyo Tsujita, Kumiko Handa, Momoyo Tsujita, Mijoko Kadewaki, Jitsuko Nishioka, Setsuko Ichimoto, Yoko Matsuda, Miyo Yamada, Terukazu Nakamura, Masakazu Takahashi, Jack Yeno Hatanaka, Taira Nishioka, Takashi Teramaye, Kikuo Nishimoto, Hideyo Takimoto, Joe Mori, Jimmie Fujimoto, Frank Toru Togami, Akio Deguchi, Toshiharu Komura, and Jack Harada.

The Alamo School on the corner of Pleasants Valley and Vaca Valley Roads was established c. 1866. In this 1910 photo are, from left to right, Lola Frasier (teacher), Sherman Bassford, Leona Woods, Marvin Woods, Doris Woods, Bernice Gates, Kathryn Gates, LaVern Gates, Meriam Vine, John Vine, Helen January, Lydia Lawrence, Margaret Lawrence, Annie Nelson, Ben Nelson, George Hinman, Ina Hinman, Walter Stark, Lida Stark, and Paul Tesson.

The Rhine School was located in Mix Canyon. In this 1906 photo are, from left to right, (front row) Susie Parrott (Sherman), Josie Bayne, Georgia Mix (Burton), Leonard Mix, Florence Parrott (Piper), Mabel Bayne, and Georgia Burton's dog Fritz; (back row) J.R. Tilson (teacher), Earl Parrot, Carl Prenkirk, and Otto Prenkirk.

The Pena School, located on Gibson Canyon Road, was established *c.* 1893. This photograph of the staff and students was taken in 1894.

This 1893 photo of Pena School and its pupils includes, from left to right, (front row) Maude Bugbee and Fred Johnson; (middle row) Harry Bugbee, Cathie Brazelton, Roth Hoyt, Walter Parks, Ernest Coleman, Fred Coleman, and the rest are unidentified; (back row) Effie Brazelton, Florence Jagers, Lynn Forsee (teacher), Alan Coleman, Pearl Brazelton, unidentified, Griffith ?, Fred Jagers, Pete Parks, and Annie Parks.

Cooper School was built about 1888. Pictured in 1959 are, from left to right, (front row) Gaynl Bera, Marilyn Hyami, Kristy Miller, and Andrea Bera; (middle row) Teddy Haskins, Stella Granado, Patsy Vasquez, Tom Bors, and teacher Mildred Burton; (back row) Stephen Vasquez and Bob Nakatani. Today Vacaville Fire Station No. 72 occupies the site at the corner of Ulatis Drive and Nut Tree Road.

This photograph was taken February 1943, but exactly when this schoolhouse, located on Browns Valley Road, was built is unknown. Construction workers at the site did find an old lumber company receipt dating back to 1918. The Browns Valley School's first classes commenced in the early 1920s.

The Browns Valley School class of 1943, from left to right, included Carol Berkstresser, Melverta Penny, Sybil Salsman, Maxine Penny, Beth Jacobs, Pearl Berkstresser, Dora Jacobs, Muriel Rogers, and Audrey Rosenbloom (on the right in front).

The last Browns Valley School year was 1962–1963. The building was sold in 1964. It was later transformed into a private home and has been continuously occupied since then.

One of the dozen or so rural district schools, the Peaceful Glen Rural School in English Hills usually had about 40 students ranging in age from 6 to 18 in this three-room building. This photo was taken c. 1910. Teacher Minnie Wagoner, standing next to the car, was known as a strict disciplinarian.

After serving the public for nearly 70 years, this is what the abandoned Peaceful Glen School looked like in 1972. Damaged by vandals, it had been moved into a nearby vacant field. On March 15, 1975, a fire destroyed what was left of the old building.

Five

THE EARLY CHURCHES

Arculus Hawkins and his wife, Cornelia, as well as James Janes, Thomas Janes, Thomas's wife, Belle, Thomas Rogers, and Mrs. McNear organized the first church in Vacaville Township on Sunday, October 4, 1854. Meetings were held in a schoolhouse near Oiler's Grove on the banks of Alamo Creek. They soon outgrew the schoolhouse, and the first church structure in Vacaville was built on the banks of Alamo Creek. Later the building was placed on rollers and towed to Catherine and Wilson Streets in Vacaville where it was used until 1891, when a new church was erected. The building served briefly as Vacaville Union High School and then was purchased by the First Presbyterian Church and moved to the corner of Wilson and East Main Streets where a fire later that year destroyed the building.

In 1891, contractor George H. Sharpe erected this new Christian church, described in the *Vacaville Reporter* as "an ornament to the town," for $4,975. In 1921 the majority of the church joined with the Baptists and Presbyterians to form the Community United Church. The superior court awarded the building to the members who joined the Community Church. In 1929 the building was sold and the money used to remodel and redecorate the Community Church. During the Depression the building was dismantled and the lumber was used to construct houses on the surrounding streets.

In 1900, the Sunday-school class met on the front steps of the Catherine Street Christian Church for a group photograph.

In 1913 the Catherine Street Christian Church began vacation Sunday school classes. Rev. A.A. Doak posed with the classes for this photo in the same year.

After the Catherine Street Christian Church was sold, the original congregation built a new structure. On January 11, 1929, the front half of a new Christian Church building on School Street was dedicated and opened to the congregation. In 1943 a rear addition was added and the front entrance remodeled. The congregation remained there until 1965 when the present church on Vine Street was built.

The first Presbyterian church in Vacaville was organized July 12, 1873, with 22 charter members. First worship services were held in the Methodist church for a few months. The congregation then purchased its first building from the Christian Church on Catherine Street and moved it to the corner of Wilson and East Main Streets. That building was destroyed by fire in 1891. A new church was built at the corner of Parker and Main Streets and dedicated on February 25, 1892. On July 11, 1909, firemen forcefully removed the steeple from the church to save the building when the Raleigh Hotel fire across the street caused it to go up in flames. The steeple was modified and repaired, and in 1912 an annex was added to the church with a large hall that could seat 450 people. After the flu epidemic of 1918, most churches suffered a serious decline in members. As a result, congregations from the Presbyterian, Baptist, and Christian Churches assembled in the Presbyterian church for service, which resulted in it becoming the Community Church of Vacaville. By 1958, the structure was in poor repair and consequently sold. Safeway Stores bought the property in 1962 and located there while the Community Church erected a new building at Eldridge and Hemlock.

The first Catholic church in Vacaville, St. Mary's, was built on Wilson Street in 1875 and was attended by a priest from Dixon. In 1898 it was moved to Catherine Street to the west and across the street from the Christian church. The church was destroyed by fire on March 12, 1925.

In 1927 fundraisers and a dance were held that netted $5,500 for a new Catholic church to be built on Merchant Street. A reinforced concrete building was completed and dedicated August 14, 1938. The church remained in use until a new one was built on the corner of Hemlock and Stinson Streets in 1956. This building served as the municipal court after some minor remodeling.

The first Japanese church in Vacaville was a Christian church consisting of a small frame building on the 500 block of Boyd Street purchased in 1897. It was named the Japanese Methodist Episcopal Church and operated until it was destroyed by fire in August 1905. The Japanese congregation then bought property on the corner of Kendal and Parker Streets for a new facility, but were unable to build because of opposition from the white citizens of Vacaville. Because there was no opposition to rebuilding on their original Boyd Street site on the outskirts of town, they built a new two-story church at the old site; the church opened in January 1909. Because feelings were running high after the bombing of Pearl Harbor and Japanese residents were being shipped to internment camps, the church was closed from 1942 to 1945. The church reopened after World War II ended, but because few Japanese returned to Vacaville, the church struggled to remain open until about 1950 when it finally closed. Members of the Japanese Methodist Episcopal Church of Vacaville gathered in front of the building for a group photo in 1927. Rev. S. Niwa was pastor at the time.

When the Japanese residents of Vacaville were relocated to internment camps, several of them stored their belongings in the Methodist Episcopal Church at 519 Boyd Street. After being released from the internment camps, only a few returned to find that the church had been vandalized and all their belongings were missing. Rev. Otoe So, who served as the pastor before the evacuation, reopened the church and had 42 members by 1948. But it was a struggle to keep operating. The church closed in 1950 and was sold to Mary "Fanney" Stewart-Kendrick, who remodeled the building into a boardinghouse with rooms for five tenants. It was a business she operated successfully for many years. In March 1998, Fanny, who was 89 at the time, fell asleep in a chair with a lit cigarette and started a devastating fire that resulted in her own death by carbon-monoxide poisoning, despite her husband's efforts to save her. The entire interior was destroyed and the building was subsequently condemned. Boarded up, it sat empty with a gaping hole in the roof, much to the chagrin of neighbors, until Joe Cook purchased the dilapidated house in 2004 with a redevelopment project consisting of six apartments in mind. "We believe this is the best use," he told commissioners, regarding his six-apartment plan. "We think it would be a nice addition to the area." The commission unanimously agreed, approving a zoning change from a single home to multi-unit housing. The Vacaville Planning Commission approved the project in February 2004 and the building will be removed to make way for the apartments.

Since only 20 percent of the Japanese in America held Christianity as their religion, a Buddhist temple was needed in Vacaville. With the aid of Clarence Uhl, property for the temple was purchased from Sam Wilson in 1910 on what is today the northeast corner of Dobbins Street and Monte Vista Avenue. The temple was built by Yoshiaki Okita for $3,975. First services were held on September 8, 1912, and the temple was formally dedicated two months later on November 3.

Children attending the Buddhist Sunday school pose on the steps of the Vacaville Japanese Temple in 1934.

When World War II ended, only a handful of Japanese returned to Vacaville from the internment camps. A few took up residence in the old Japanese Buddhist temple and school that were then being used as boarding houses, the only buildings remaining of Japanese origin in town. On November 23, 1951, a raging fire destroyed the temple. Two men, Fukiumatsu Tsujimoto and Seiichi Yukawa, were seriously burned in the inferno, which was believed to have been started by a kerosene heater explosion. Tsujimoto later died from his injuries. Because so few Japanese remained in the area, the temple was never rebuilt.

Located at the Elmira Cemetery are two monuments to remind passersby of the once-thriving Japanese population in Vacaville. To the left is the San Gai Ban Rei stone that was once located at the Buddhist church and on the right is the E Ko Jo Sho stone placed there in May 1957 in memory of Vacaville's Japanese citizens.

The abandoned Seventh Day Adventist Church in a residential area at 501 Elizabeth Street is little known to most Vacaville residents. It was constructed on Lot 1, Block G of Parker's 1884 addition to the town of Vacaville. The subdivision included eight-and-a-half blocks on the south side of Vacaville on land that Parker bought from Mason and Luzena Wilson for $125 per acre in 1882. The parcel was surveyed and subdivided in 1884 into lots that measured 134 by 50 feet. The Pacific Sabbatanan Association Inc. (Seventh Day Adventist Church) purchased the lot on the corner of Elizabeth and Stevenson Streets in 1891 from the W.B. Parker Company for $250. This wooden church, erected in the same year, is the only 19th-century church left standing in the Vacaville area.

Four

EVENTS IN
VACAVILLE'S GROWTH

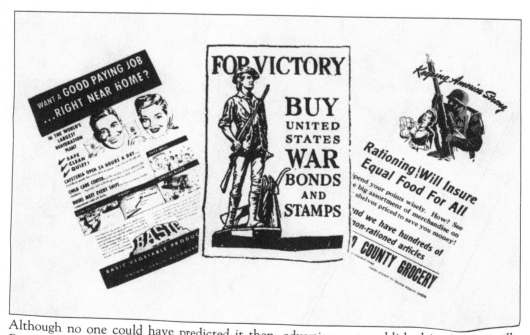

Although no one could have predicted it then, advertisements published in the Vacaville *Reporter* for Basic Foods and posters for World War II were the first indication that the still small town of Vacaville, with a total population of 1,608 in 1940, was about to experience explosive growth.

After Pearl Harbor was bombed in 1941, feelings toward Japanese Americans rapidly deteriorated. On April 26, 1942, Civilian Exclusion Order No. 23 was issued, commanding "all persons of Japanese ancestry, both alien and non-alien" to be removed from Solano County by noon, Sunday, May 3, 1942. This left little time to dispose of or store personal property and belongings owned by the hapless Japanese. On May 2, Solano County's Japanese Americans boarded a train for the Turlock processing center.

Some of Vacaville's Japanese citizens were interred at the camp at Gila River, Arizona. Vacaville's Tomio Teraura (second row on left) is shown here, c. 1943, working in a shop where model ships used to teach ship identification were made. After the war, very few of Vacaville's Japanese citizens returned to the town they had once called home.

Scrap metal, rubber, plastic, and other materials were a vital need during the war. Vacaville was quick to comply with drives to collect the scrap shown here in the Safeway parking lot at the corner of Dobbins and Main Streets.

Throughout World War II, Vacaville citizens scoured the skies 24 hours a day for enemy aircraft from this Vine Street Civil Defense tower on the Buckley Ranch.

93

Victory rallies were an important function in the effort to sell war bonds and stamps. The Vacaville High School band provided entertainment for this rally in front of the Vacaville Theater in 1943.

Two days after receiving news of the victory at Iwo Jima in 1945, Vacaville celebrated with a parade down Main Street.

News of victory in Europe spread fast as Vacaville citizens gathered in front of the post office on Main Street to get the word and celebrate.

It was in the postwar years that Vacaville's population flourished, even while remnants of wartime housing lingered on. This southerly aerial view shows Highway 40 (now Interstate 80) running across the top of the photo. The first major subdivision in Vacaville (top left) was Vaca Valley Village, constructed in the mid-1940s. Just to the right is Vaca Valley Acres, "temporary" wartime housing that was later purchased by the City of Vacaville. The city rented the "units" for several years until they were torn down to make room for the present city hall complex.

Ever since Vacaville was founded in 1851, citizens of the community have served as firemen, from the days of the bucket brigade to the present age of high-powered fire engines. Throughout those years various temporary housing for the equipment was provided by frame buildings and tin sheds, but it wasn't until 1957 that the Vacaville Fire Department had a building of its own. Planning for Vacaville's new firehouse started with the appointment of a planning board in 1955. Three committees—equipment, finance, and building—were selected, and in 1956 San Mateo architect Albert W. Kahl was hired by Vacaville City Council to draw the plans for the new building. A bid of $64,500 was received when the project was let out to bidders, and since this was more than the community wanted to spend, the council and the Vacaville Fire Department joined hands to proceed with the structure as a local project. Actual work started on the site on November 3, 1956, and by late 1957 the project was completed. Vacaville's volunteer firemen contributed over 3,000 man-hours of labor while other civic-minded citizens and organizations added another 500 man-hours. The building was financed without issuance of bonds or increases in taxes. The cost of the structure, sidewalks, and ramps totaled $46,000 and represented a considerable saving to the taxpayers. From its treasury, the Vacaville Fire Department purchased about $6,000 worth of furnishings. The building served as headquarters until 1997 and was later removed to make way for the senior center.

OPPOSITE, BELOW: During a quiet evening on May 14, 1964, the sound of a small explosion in an abandoned sheet metal shop on the corner of East Main and McClellan Streets startled nearby residents. Firemen soon discovered the explosion came from a 400-gallon still whose tubes had clogged during its first cook of mash. It wasn't hard to summon the police since this was then the heart of downtown and the police department was located two blocks down the street in the old town hall. Along with the still, Vacaville police found 328 gallons of crude alcohol, which apparently had been strained from mash at another location, according to the chief. Apparently only one gallon had been processed when the short-lived operation literally blew its cover.

In 1957 the Vacaville police force and justice court was still housed in the old town hall on East Main Street. The officers at the time, from left to right, were Fellers, Langford, Ashcroft, Young, Pore, DeGracia, Gray, McCord, Lanqua, Taylor, and Hallmark.

By 1961 Vacaville's population had grown by almost 750 percent since 1940, when it only had 1,608 citizens. VIPs posed by the 1961 city limit sign that proclaimed Vacaville had a population of 10,898.

As Vacaville grew, a major roadblock was solved in 1962 when opening ceremonies for the Monte Vista Bridge over Ulatis Creek joined North Street with Callen Street (later Monte Vista) and became East and West Monte Vista Avenue.

The Vaca Valley Creamery, shown here in 1967, was a favorite hangout of local teenagers for many years. It closed in November 1970 and was occupied by miscellaneous shops until the building was demolished in 2003 to make way for downtown redevelopment.

With the population exploding, the old Carnegie Library could no longer adequately serve Vacaville. A new library was authorized and funded and is shown here in the process of being built to the left of city hall in 1969.

The Hargis House on now defunct College Street was in the process of being demolished on January 26, 1970, when this photo was taken, so that Andrews Park and Ulatis Park could be joined. William Schroeder built the house in 1906 on the site of the former cemetery of today's Andrews Park, then sold it to Dr. Louis Marshall, whose widow sold it to Harold Hargis. The Hargis family and Art Dietz built a meat locker and butcher shop in the basement. Local hunters used the facility and at times as many as eight deer were hanging in the cold storage room.

Vacaville improvements in 1970 included widening Merchant Street from Cernon to Parker as well as removing the crown from the street.

With its increasing population, Vacaville needed to upgrade its old sewer system. Improvements from Main Street out to the Dobbins/Deodora Street area in 1972 caused temporary inconvenience to local businesses in 1972. The following year the sewer system was extended to Fruitvale Avenue to serve new home developments.

By 1972 the majority of development had taken place to the north of Interstate 80. In the center is the new Vacaville High School on Monte Vista Avenue and the Vine Street hills appear in the background.

The beginning of development on the south side of Interstate 80 in 1972 can be seen by the outline where the Vacaville (later Three Oaks) Community Center was to be built. Most of the areas south of the highway were still orchard land at this time.

The new Vacaville Community Center and Swimming Pool opened December 1, 1973, on Alamo Street and was still surrounded by orchards. The center was later renamed Three Oaks Community Center. This photo, taken before the community center parking lot was added, shows the community center in the upper center and the swimming pool in the lower left.

An unidentified man cleans up after the ceiling at Amphlett's home and decorating store caved in on November 27, 1976. High winds knocked a vent from its moorings, forcing air into the top of the ceiling where several feet of pigeon droppings and dead birds had built up between the ceiling and roof. Owner Jack Amphlett was out of town when it happened, but employee Fran Ottinger (above) had to crawl out from under the debris, luckily unhurt. The loss was estimated between $5,000 and $10,000. The original building, constructed in 1883, is the oldest structure still standing in Vacaville's historic downtown district. Owned by Carleton Crystal, it was at one time occupied by Wells Fargo before Amphlett moved into it in 1968.

Before celebrating Vacaville's heritage became an annual event known as Fiesta Days, local residents celebrated Vacaville's centennial. Early celebrants in the upper photo, from left to right, included (front row) John Lorenzo, unidentified, Maria Dolores Lyon (granddaughter of Manuel Vaca), Eleanor Nelson, and Robert Heffernan; (middle row) Frank Tortosa, John Rico, James McCrory, Nestora Lyon, Otto Meyers, Alfred Johnson, and Kathleen Heffernan; (back row) Edger Tucker and Cy Maloney. In 1980, the Fiesta Days Parade included outstanding floats and entertainment, which can be seen heading down Main Street in the photo to the left.

Seven

MODERN DAYS
CONNECT TO THE PAST

Local Historian Bob Allen studies a wall of Huey's Pub that has historic roots in Vacaville. After the fire of 1895 destroyed all the buildings on the north side of Main Street, this structure was built with bricks to address growing fire prevention concerns. The bricks were retrieved from the old college that had been on School Hill (now Andrews Park) from 1865 to 1895. In the new structure, the bricks have been left exposed to fit in with the theme of the Vacaville's historic downtown district. The building served first as the Louvre Restaurant, followed by a feed store, five and dime store, the Buckhorn Bar, and Phelan's Lounge.

Improvements continue in 2004 on the north side of East Main Street near the Ulatis Bridge. The Firefalls Restaurant on the corner next to Ulatis Bridge dates from the 1930s and is now an upscale restaurant with views overlooking the Andrews Park Creekwalk.

Vacaville's heritage is reflected in a mural on the Heritage Café, which occupies the lot where the original Pony Express stop was located in the old E.F. Gillespie Store built in 1854.

This photo, taken from the front of the Heritage Café, shows construction on the new plaza. In the background the new library is being built. A mural depicting Vacaville history will be painted inside the building. In the foreground is a monument marking the area of the Pony Express station.

Vacaville City Hall proudly displays its local history through the use of designer tiles on a wall in front of the council chambers.

With Vacaville in the throes of escalating growth, the city council of 1984–1986 had to make many hard decisions on how to handle the downtown business district. The council, from left to right, included Mike Connor, Robert Pokorney, Mayor Dave Fleming, Bill Carroll, and David Lowe. Dave Fleming and Bill Carroll were the driving forces in establishing the downtown area as a historic district.

Vacaville's 2004–2005 city council has a delicate balancing act to perform in maintaining the historic downtown business district along with several redevelopment projects in the works. The council, from left to right, includes Steve Wilkins, Pauline Clancy, Len Augustine, Steve Hardy, and Rischa Slade.

The old town hall, built in 1907 after the Vacaville jailhouse—a small shed with two cells—was shoved into Ulatis Creek, houses the Vacaville Heritage Council and its archive of history and photographs on the lower floor and the Solano County Genealogy Society and its extensive library and records on the upper level.

The KUIC Plaza, next door to the old town hall, is a modern building housing radio station KUIC-FM and office space on the site of the first Akerly's General Store.

F.A. Steiger, who designed the old town hall, also designed the Ulatis Bridge, which was also known as the School Street Bridge and built in 1911. The view (below) shows the crossing onto School Street that is now the main entrance to Andrews Park.

Vacaville takes great pride in its
Andrews Park and Creekwalk. In
the upper photograph is a view
toward the Ulatis Bridge and the
entertainment center with its
"surprise" fountain that randomly
spouts water from the ground.
Concerts, entertainment, and
special functions are held here
during summer months. On the right
is a small portion of the Creekwalk
with its winding path along the
Ulatis Creek below Andrews Park.

A waterfall flowing from the edge of Andrews Park under the Creekwalk provides a pleasant place to relax on a hot day.

History buffs can learn about Vacaville's history from kiosks scattered around Andrews Park. The kiosks are maintained by members of the Vacaville Heritage Council under the direction of the Vacaville City Council. They feature historic photographs and snippets of information about the nearby historic district.

Still known as the "Opera House" at 560 Main Street, this building was constructed in 1897 by Sidney Walker and originally housed stores on the ground floor and the opera house upstairs. When the Barcar building burned in 1939, the Masonic Lodge relocated to the upper floor of the opera house. Today it is used for special occasions and catered lunches. Active Styles Health Club occupies the lower floor.

TJ's Tavern at 554 Main was built in 1897 as Arnold and Bugbees Hardware Store and was also at one time a J.C. Penney store. Today's Cocoannie's Fashion Store at 548 Main Street started life in 1890 as Hacke's Hardware, later became Winfield Hardware, and more recently PG&E and Brooks Tavern. Micro Dynamic Computers at 542 Main Street served as the Vacaville Bank until 1920.

The International Order of Odd Fellows was organized in Vacaville in the 1850s. The original meeting place was on the northwest corner of Main and Elizabeth Streets and was destroyed by fire in 1877. After the fire the IOOF acquired the present site at 534–536 Main Street. In 1884 fire again destroyed their wooden structure. In 1889 the present building was constructed, this time out of brick. The idea of using brick was to make the building more fireproof, but the entire facade was toppled into the street by the earthquake of 1892. The facade was rebuilt and remains the same today. Currently the Margarito Barber Shop and the Fiesta Days Office occupy the lower floor.

Today, a tattoo parlor occupies this building at 528 Main Street. The structure was built right after a devastating fire destroyed most of the downtown area in 1888. It was constructed for McWilliam's Grocery and became Page's Grocery Store in 1895. In the early 1900s, F. Bissel's Dry Goods occupied it, as did a barbershop.

This was originally a wooden building that housed Bennett's Saloon until November 1888 when a fire destroyed most of the south side of Main Street. Bennett rebuilt using brick, and today this site is home to the Mary Cornelison Photography Shop. Bennett's Saloon was rated one of the finest parlors in Solano County with stained-glass front windows and the finest paneling available inside. It did a booming business, and Bennett later was quoted as being in favor of Vacaville's incorporation, "as long as license fees were raised to $1,000 a year to keep disreputable places out of business." Today Bennett's building is easily recognizable because his initials are prominently displayed in the top of the front wall: "ELB."

The building, housing the Tamazula Mexican Restaurant and Jackson's Medical Supply at 506 A and B Main Street, was built in 1885 by S.C. Walker, the same person who built the opera house. Blum's Mercantile first occupied the building, followed by the United Cigar Company. During the 1910s it served as the Central Movie Theater and later Shock's Country Oak Store.

This fine building at 500 Main Street was built for the Bank of Vacaville in 1920. Later it became the Bank of Italy, which evolved into the Bank of America. Today it is the home of law offices and still has the original safe.

The Lopez family has operated Barber Joe's in this building since 1940. It was constructed in 1902 for the Riechers and Atchison Meat Market on the site of one of the first buildings constructed in Vacaville, which had been destroyed in the 1888 fire.

Built in 1897 by R.L. Reid at 438 Main Street, this building first served as Reid's Drug Store and T.L. Hewitt's Jewelry Store both in the same room. Before today's Silk n Crafts store moved in it was occupied by the Vacaville Institute of Tae Kwan Do.

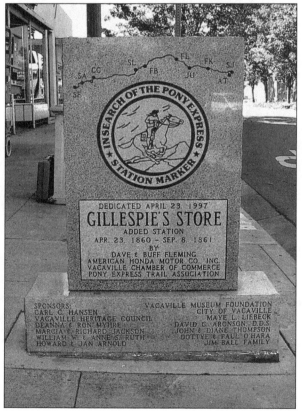

The Heritage House Restaurant occupies the original location of the E.F. Gillespie Store that was built in 1854 and was one of the first merchandise stores to open in Vacaville. In 1857 Wells Fargo opened an express and post office agency in the same building, with E.F. Gillespie as the agent. In addition, the building served as a Pony Express stop in 1865. The Gillespie store fell into disrepair and was gone before 1897.

This building was constructed in 1897 for the L.B. Peterson Cash Store. Subsequent tenants have included Barclay and Peterson, Barclay and Ream, the Safeway Store in 1928, Star Bakery, Lorraine Restaurant, and today's Heritage House Café. A monument dedicated to the Pony Express sponsored by the citizens and organizations of Vacaville was dedicated on April 23, 1997, to mark the historic location.

Located at 307 Main, this unusually shaped building was constructed in 1897 by Joseph Lagler and was also part of the Star Bakery. It was later used as the Vacaville Bakery and, in the early 1900s, as the Vienna Bakery owned by Karl Kopp. More recently it was occupied by the King Pin Trophy store and today is the Eagle Eye Engraving shop.

The well-known Triangle Building occupies the entire 400 block of Main Street. Unique in Vacaville, it was built in 1898 and is located at the intersections of Merchant, Main, and Dobbins Streets. Many important businesses occupied it over the years, including the telephone company, First National Bank of Vacaville, the *Reporter* newspaper, and the Vacaville Drug Store. The original bank vault is still located inside. Today Ray's Bicycle Shop and Kappel & Kappel Real Estate occupy the lower floor.

In 1992 the Vacaville Centennial Commission appointed Lisa Reinertson to craft this statue, *The Fruit Pickers*, to celebrate Vacaville's100th year since incorporation. It was placed at the corner of Merchant and Main Streets in front of the Triangle Building and formally dedicated September 23, 1995.

Known as the Crystal Building, Vacaville's oldest brick building has withstood the many disasters of time. Although it appears to be three different buildings, Platt and Stick General Merchandise built it as a single structure in 1883. Over time it has served as Crystal Brothers Dry Goods, Schaefer's Big Country Store, and later Lloyd Chandler's Furniture. At the time of the 1892 earthquake, the post office was also located in the rear of the building. Today, Amphlett's Interiors, Main Street Salon, and Tux n' Tailor occupy the building at 354, 350, and 344 Main Street, respectively.

Raleigh Barcar, who published the *Vacaville Reporter* in the 1890s, built the Barcar Building in 1898 and published the newspaper in one of the sections. A social club known as the Ulatis Club was upstairs in the early days. The structure also contained the Grand Theater, later known as the Strand Theater, on the left side from the 1910s to the 1920s. The Vacaville Fire Department, Coffman's Candies, California Market, Collier's Bowling Alley, a millinery shop, and the Cole & Chandler Dress Shop were also located here in the 1920s and 1930s. Fire extensively damaged the building on January 23, 1942, and today it no longer reflects the old style of construction it had before the fire.

The Clark Theater opened in 1929 and initially showed silent movies. The name was changed to Vacaville Theater in 1931. Although still standing, it no longer functions as a theater.

In 1904 the Women's Improvement Club and the Ulatis Book Club applied to the Carnegie Foundation for $5,000 to construct a public library. In 1912 a tax was approved to maintain a public library and the Carnegie Foundation upped their offer to $12,000 if the city provided a lot. Construction was completed in 1914 and the building was used as the public library until 1970. Several businesses have occupied the building over the years and today the Vacaville Chamber of Commerce at 300 Main Street is located there.

Vacaville's first permanent post office was built in 1937 at 301 Main Street, complete with a full basement. Since the post office closing in the 1960s, the building has been occupied by a liquor store and several restaurants. Today the Old Post Office Seafood and Grill occupies the building.

One of the few remaining historic buildings on the north side of Main Street first belonged to Heinrich's Meat Market, which opened in 1897. Today the China House Restaurant calls this 513 Main Street address home.

This building at 519 Main Street was built after the fire of 1895 with bricks from the California College, located in Andrews Park from 1865 to 1895. It was first operated as the Louvre Restaurant, then a feed store, a 5-10-25¢ store and, in the 1930s, the Buckhorn Bar. More recently it was home to Phelan's Lounge and now Huey's Pub.

Vacaville proudly extends protection to many buildings and objects, such as this huge black walnut tree, which was planted around 1886. Located on the Wykoff Ranch, it supplied the seeds and cuttings for over 100 orchards in the area and is protected by deed from being cut down until it dies of natural causes.

"UNCLE BURT'S TREE"

VACAVILLE

This famous Black Walnut tree has provided the nuts for starting over 100 walnut groves in California. It gave shade for travelers and their teams who enjoyed the Wykoff Ranch hospitality of the cool well water nearby. It is said to have been planted when Burt Wykoff (1886-1977) was born. Uncle Burt deeded that the tree is to remain in place until it dies. Uncle Burt is now gone, but his tree lives on.

Plaque dedicated year 2002
Vacaville Historical Marker Committee

The people of Vacaville have long been interested in their local history, but that enthusiasm does not stop at the city limits. In the late 1970s, the idea of building a county museum in Vacaville emerged. Bolstered by the donation of a lot next to her mansion on Buck Avenue by Eva Buck, widow of Sen. Frank H. Buck Jr., and cash donations, several citizens started the ball rolling. Ground for the museum was broken in 1981. Early museum board members responsible for overseeing the project were board president John McBride, Nut Tree owner Robert Power, Barbara Martell Comfort, Arlene King Pillsbury, Judge Walter Wier, and councilman David Fleming, who later became mayor of Vacaville. Volunteers who contributed a great deal of time and effort included Vacaville historians Bert Hughes, Robert Allen, Jane LoPolito, and Carroll Mundy. The doors opened in May 1983 to the delight of many visitors. Major collections of artifacts and photographs from throughout the county have been placed under the museum's care. The excellent oversight of longtime director Ruth Begell came to an end when, after serving 15 years from 1985 until 2000, she was appointed director of the Charles Schultz Museum in Santa Rosa. The Vacaville Museum has continued to thrive under the able leadership of museum director Shawn Lum. The many exciting historical exhibits and activities depicting life throughout Solano County are a credit to her skills and hard-working staff.

The William Henry Buck home across the street from the Vacaville Museum on the corner of Buck Avenue and Kentucky Street is a fine example of the many historic homes that line the avenue. George Sharpe built this stately home in 1892 for $5,000. Sharpe also built the Presbyterian church in 1891, Vacaville High School in 1898, Vacaville Grammar School in 1909, and the Carnegie Library in 1915. The house was totally renovated inside and out in 2003.

These palms on the left side of Buck Avenue have thrived since they were planted in 1902. They provide pleasant shade for the interested stroller who wanders along Buck Avenue to admire the stately mansions from the 19th and 20th centuries.

For years, people could literally smell Vacaville while traveling down Interstate 40 and later Interstate 80. The Basic Vegetable Company started small in 1933 and became one of Vacaville's main employers for 53 years when it moved to Davis Street in the 1950s. Its mainstay was dehydrating onions, the odor of which spread over the area with a vengeance, causing many travelers to hunger for a good old American hamburger. That is until 1986, when the company closed its doors and moved to another town.

One of Vacaville's biggest employers, and a landmark for 75 years, shut down in 1996. In early 2004 the bulldozers moved in and leveled the Nut Tree to the ground. On March 1, 2004, all that remained was the battered shell of the famous Nut Tree sign.

Three icons that have consistently been identified with Vacaville are the Nut Tree, the Pena Adobe, and the old town hall. The Nut Tree was so well known that often people could tell you where it was located but, when asked, wouldn't know where Vacaville was. Vacaville began life with the Vacas and the Penas and the Pena Adobe is a reminder of the town's historic roots. Today the adobe is part of a community park in Lagoon Valley and has its own small museum. Although currently not open to the public on a regular basis, future development in Lagoon Valley may provide the funds and administration for a full-time curator. The old town hall, originally a fire station, a jail, and a court, is still used as a repository for local history and genealogy. The Pena Adobe and the old town hall survived but, sadly, the Nut Tree is no more and the property will soon be redeveloped.

Printed in the USA
CPSIA information can be obtained
at www.ICGtesting.com
LVHW071052231123
764526LV00015BA/13